To
Dr Joh...

CW00705401

RUNNING CHRONICLES

Copyright © 2021 Nana Ofori-Atta Oguntola

ISBN: 9798777810380

Cover Design: We Are Creative (WAC)

Written by Nana Ofori-Atta Oguntola

Email: nanaooguntola@gmail.com

Website: nanaoguntola.me

@ nanaoforiattaoguntola

Published by VINASHA Productions

www.vinasha.org

Best wishes
Happy Running

1

CONTENTS

Chapter One: You Inspire   4

Chapter Two: It's No Cliché   7

Chapter Three: The Right Tools   12

Chapter Four: Run In The Rain   15

Chapter Five: Cry If I Want To   17

Chapter Six: The Destination Awaits   21

Chapter Seven: Habits Are Hard To Break   24

Chapter Eight: Don't Mind The Rain   28

Chapter Nine: The Faithful Custodian   32

Chapter Ten: Settle In For A Marathon   37

Chapter Eleven: Find Time For Solitude   40

Chapter Twelve: Becoming You   43

Chapter Thirteen: Grandma's Lesson   48

Chapter Fourteen: Results   51

Chapter Fifteen: Set The Pace   53

Chapter Sixteen: Who's Watching   56

Chapter Seventeen: The Price   59

Chapter Eighteen: Confidence Boost   62

Chapter Nineteen: The Naysayers   65

Chapter Twenty: Kick The Clichés   67

Chapter Twenty One: Your Biggest Cheerleader   71

The Bonus Track: Grow In The Pain   73

The Bonus Track: Don't Stay The Same   75

About The Author   77

1

YOU INSPIRE

Sometimes when I go running, I go past a group of two, three or four women walking for their exercise.

I would run round one lap and go past them walking, then, I'll run a second lap and go past them still walking.

Inevitably, by the time I come round for my third or fourth lap one or more members of the group would have broken off and started running as I come close.

On other occasions it might be a man or a couple of men walking. Once they see me go round once or twice, they also begin to run quite aggressively and then they get tired very quickly and stop.

They, however, endeavour to make sure they are running each time I am getting close so that I see them running.

This made me think about how we inspire people. We do not necessarily go out to say 'I am an inspiration I will inspire people'.

Our actions, however, are what inspire. Whether we know the people or have no interactions with them, once we keep running, we never know how those actions can inspire other people to do something good for themselves.

People say to me 'you inspire me, or you motivate me'. Most times I am surprised because I just do what I do without thinking how it might affect other people. But it does, because people watch what you do whether you are conscious of it or not.

I have also learnt that people might not like you, they might resent you and still be inspired by you. Sometimes you might be able to see how much of what you do is replicated in their lives without them acknowledging your influence. Remember that sometimes imitation is always the best form of flattery.

Additionally, if I am not inspired or motivated, I will not challenge others to do the same. In the same vein, if you are not motivated or inspired yourself, you cannot inspire or motivate others. No amount of talking will make up for actually doing something. Words mean nothing if people cannot see your actions.

Your inspiration is to yourself first and to others second.

#keeprunning

#youcannotinspire
ifyouarenotinspired

#inspire

2

IT'S NO CLICHÉ

There have been several occasions when I am running and get to a point where it feels like I cannot just take another step. I am exhausted and I feel like I must stop for a minute.

Everything hurts at this point. All my muscles feel like they are being pulled and stretched and twisted. It's agony.

Experience has taught me however, that if I keep placing one foot in front of the other and keep running, the pain will pass, and I'll forget it even hurts.

I have learnt that I can push past the pain because I have done it a few times before. I have learnt that the pain will not kill me. Beyonce described it once as 'We bend, we do not break'.

In fact, I have learnt that relief comes to those parts of my body that felt stretched and pulled and twisted if I just keep running.

And so, I keep running and after a while I realise that I had stopped hurting a while back and I had not even noticed when the pain stopped.

The same applies to life. Sometimes I get to a point, and everything hurts so bad. I don't want to wake up, I don't want to work, I don't want to take another step. There is so much that has gone wrong or not gone the way I would like it to go, and I feel like I will collapse with the next step.

Recently I described my business as 'having gone to visit hell for the summer'. No money was coming in, just rising bills.

That was truly painful: Getting up to face the day, to work, to talk to my children was hard. I had to keep talking to clients, creating new business opportunities, engaging with communities, implementing new projects right through the pain.

My experience has taught me however that none of this will last forever: That if I just get up from the bed, if I just keep working, If I just put one foot in front of another and keep going, this moment, this pain will pass.

I might have no money now, I might be totally stressed by family, work can be going slowly, clients are not coming in but if I only keep going, I will find myself go past this moment and then without even realising it I will turn around and the moment will be behind me.

I find that I have stretched and grown in the areas in which there was pain. I have learnt lessons. I have become better and healthier, emotionally and mentally.

It is not easy to keep going. It is not a cliché or a flippant statement to make. The alternative is to give up and that is not an option. You cannot reach your destination if you stop now.

Sometimes it can get so dark you are not sure where to place your foot for the next step. But you must take the step-in the dark- and keep moving.

One thing I have learnt: The fire always burns itself to ashes. The storm always passes. The writing on the wall always says, 'Woman Thou Art Whole'.

#neverstop

#nevergiveup

#itsonlyforamoment

#keepworking

#hustlebaby

#fightforit

#pushthroughthepain

#keepgoing

3

THE RIGHT TOOLS

I had my running shoes for three or four years and then they developed a hole at the top. I knew I wanted to buy a new one, but I just kept putting it off. In the first instance I did not want to deal with the hassle of having to look through shoes and choose one.

After all I could still run in them, so I run with the hole in the shoe for at least four months.

Then for my birthday, my son bought me new running shoes- nicer ones than I would have bought for myself.

Just because I did not have the perfect tools to do the job does not mean I should stop running.

They might let water sip in and create some discomfort whilst I run. I most certainly deserve a new shoe.

The current tools and equipment and circumstances might not be right. They might not look good. People might look at them and see their inadequacy and ugliness.

None of that means I should stop running in the interim. I don't stay home and say I need new running shoes and so I will not run till I get them.

No! I run in the shoes I have till the new ones come along. Whether I buy them, or they are given to me. The important thing here is to focus and keep running. The tools might be inadequate, but they allow me to run. So, I must use them until I can get better ones.

Similarly I did not know there was a 'good' way to run. It's just running after all so I just went out and ran.

After years of running, someone told me the 'good' way to run is to land on my toes, as landing on your heels does damage to your knee.

So now that I knew better, I changed my running style and started landing on my toes. This engaged new muscles and caused some discomfort for a while but I settled into it and that became my new way of running.

In the same way if you don't have the right tools, skills, equipment, people, money to support your work or vision, keep your eye on the purpose and keep working and running in what you have available to you now.

You don't say *'I have to wait till I have the right tools or technique or money or people to run'*. Start right where you are. Use what you have.

Don't stop working or pushing or believing. Keep running until the right tools turn up because they always will.

If you remain faithful to where you are and what you have, the right tools will come to take you to the next level.

Do better when you know better.

#Keeprunning

#keepdoingthework

#focusonpurpose

4

RUN IN THE RAIN

It rained for three days in a row. Every day I woke up to run it was raining and I'd cancel my run.

Then on day four I decided that was enough and went running despite the rain.

It was wet, but I did run. Nothing bad happened to me and I completed my run.

The right circumstances will not always turn up so that you can do what you want to do. Do it anyway. Get out there in the rain and work. You will be stronger for it.

Your self-esteem will go up. You will feel more confident that you pushed through the barriers and finally you would have achieved your goal despite the obstacles.

#Letitrain

#workanyway

#workintherain

#runintherain

#danceintherain

5
CRY IF I WANT TO

I don't remember what happened, but it was upsetting enough to have me cry. As I run in the rain, the tears ran freely down my face.

It didn't matter that I was crying in public as I run because no one could see my tears. There is a liberation in that moment when you can cry openly.

As the rain washed away my tears it also brought the healing and the peace I needed to make at the moment with whatever had upset me.

A lot of times we hurt, and no one sees our pain. We have become so accomplished at keeping our pain and tears hidden from people.

However, it is important to cry our tears because there is healing in our tears. It is important to acknowledge the pain and release the hurt.

Society makes us embarrassed to cry. It shows weakness and nobody has time for weak people. Society is all about the strongest and the winner who takes all.

It is untrue that we can be strong all the time. It is important that we allow the weakness in sometimes, so we don't become hardened and cynical and unable to empathise with others.

Crying not only brings the healing and relief we need. It makes us stronger and better. So let the tears flow sometimes- when you need to.

#crying

#healing

#rain

#bestronger

#bewiser

6

THE DESTINATION AWAITS

When I leave the house to go for a run, I know my final destination is to go back home. I can get tired on the way; I can use a longer route or a different one, but my mind is locked into the fact that I am running back home.

Sometimes I get to a point - usually going uphill- and I feel the pain. The thighs hurt, I get too hot and all I want to do is stop.

Or it might be that I have not run for a few days and I start running again, oh the agony.

But then I think, 'I left home for a reason'. I have a purpose and destination. I set out to run and to run back home. That is what I must do. I remind myself why I set out in the first place.

If I stop running, I will not get to my destination. My destination is there waiting for me to get to it. I can only do that if I keep running towards it.

There is a clear view of my destination in my mind, I know exactly where I am headed. So, I keep running till I get back home and by so doing fulfil my mission.

It's the same with life. There are times when it seems impossible. This aim cannot be achieved. The pain is too great.

But remind yourself why you started running in the first place. What was the purpose you set out to achieve? Renew your objective, remember your vision, your purpose and keep running.

It's the same with business. There is a destination. It must be as clear, as tangible and as real as the house you are running towards.

You might get tired given how challenging life is. There will be obstacles and troubles. You might take longer than you planned. You might change the route or plan you originally had to get there.

If, however, you keep the destination clearly in your mind and keep running I believe you will get there.

Set your vision once more in clear view before you and don't stop moving. It is there waiting for you. You simply need to keep running towards it.

#keeprunning

#drivenbypurpose

#purposedrivenlife

#dontstopnow

7
HABITS ARE HARD TO BREAK

I travelled to Scotland for a Spa weekend with my girlfriends. I took my running clothes but forgot to take my running shoe. So, the next morning I was up at 4am out of habit. Out of habit I started working.

This is what I normally did at home and so even though I was on holiday my body did what it always did and woke up at 4am.

When it was time to run at 6am I got changed into my running clothes and that's when I realised I had not brought my shoes.

I guess I could have just jumped back into bed, but my mind had so been wired into running I could not. My body and mind were in unison, 'you have to run'.

So, I put on the soft shoes I had brought for walking around in and took off.

We were on a golf course and the paths were stony. Sometimes the stones hurt so much I would run on the grass verges. Those were soggy and unpleasant and so back onto the hard, stony ground I went. My run was shorter than normal. No more than twenty minutes.

When I told my friends they said you are on holiday, it's okay to rest. Don't cause yourself too much discomfort by running'.

The next day routine kicked into gear again. This time I had decided I would not run.

Then a funny situation happened in my head where I had to convince my body and my own mind to step down: That today I would not run. That it was okay for me not to run. I had to explain that I was on holiday and it was just for a few days and it was too uncomfortable and it was okay to stay in bed for a couple of extra hours.

Watching myself have this conversation with myself was interesting.

I learnt two lessons from this experience:

1. Whatever I train my body and mind to do is exactly what it would do. Once a habit kicks in it is hard to break. Grow good habits.

2. I learnt that I could run in less comfortable shoes. Sometimes we must work in less comfortable situations: In areas, with people, in places and situations which we are not used to and which stretch us.

If we keep running, we can still achieve our goals. We need to learn to adjust and adapt and change and flow and we will complete the task.

#goodhabits

#growgoodhabits

#mindconditioning

#runanyway

#change

#adapt

#stretch

8

DON'T MIND THE RAIN

It's raining but I have not run for a few days. My body and mind are restless. We need to run. It's a habit I have developed over the years and habits are hard to break.

So, as I looked out of the window at the rain, I said to myself; 'The rain is doing what it must. It is rain. It must rain.

I, on the hand, I must do what I must. I must run. What has the rain to do with my running?'

I got changed and went out for my run in the rain, for the rain is not my concern.

The parable of the sower talks about the farmer who went to plant seeds. Some fell on stony ground, some fell among thorns, some were eaten by the birds.

Does that mean he should stop sowing? No, because some will fall on good ground and bear much fruit and provide a harvest beyond the seeds sown.

The difficulties, the challenges, the problems they must come. That's who they are. It's what they do. By their nature and nomenclature, they are fulfilling their own purpose. They can be relentless, almost unending.

You stand there looking at them and wondering if they will ever end. Like the rain, they are a constant 'pitter patter' against your window.

You and I must go out and keep running. What have the problems and obstacles got to do with our running?

They may look insurmountable like they would blind us but if we can keep our eyes on the prize, we will run right through them.

Our job is to keep running and keep pursuing vision. Our job is to remain focused on what we need to do and let the problems alone to do what they do.

In the end the rain stops anyway. It does not rain forever. It has a time limit, an expiration date and so do the problems and obstacles you face.

#keeprunning

#obstaclescant stopyou

#problemsdontlast

#letitrain

#runanyway

9

THE FAITHFUL CUSTODIAN

One day, as I was running, I started thinking about the Parable of the talents told by Jesus in the Bible.

He tells the story where a master gives one servant five talents, another three and the third, one.

When the Master returns and asks the servants to give account of the talents he had given them one said 'you gave me five I now have ten', the second said 'you gave me three I now have six' and the third said 'because I fear you I hid mine away, here it is'.

I know the parallel to the use of talents has been made on countless occasions, however as I meditated on this parable on my run I came up with another interpretation.

I liken the talents given to the servants to wealth and money and power and privilege and opportunity.

The first one finds five others he can mentor to be like him. He supports them financially, emotionally and helps them to be as wealthy and as powerful as him. What would then happen is that each of these five would go out and find another five to mentor and reproduce themselves in.

Then twenty-five people become millionaires who mentor another five and they continue to grow outward. A powerful interlinked network of millionaires and people of influence.

When the master calls this original servant to account, he has reproduced his talent and himself many times over. He can proudly say this is what I have done, and he will be praised.

The second servant does the same and mentors and supports and reproduces himself in many others. His master will also be proud of him.

The third one however comes in and says well, I bought my cars, and my houses, I invested in stocks and bonds. I am well off and all the money you gave me is in the bank safe and sound.

I have not mentored or reproduced myself in anyone as I did not want anyone to use me or to waste my money. All I return to you is myself.

Who will the master be pleased with?

We are not on earth to accumulate wealth for ourselves and our children alone. We are here to reproduce ourselves as many times as we can.

God's first commandment to man was to reproduce. We do not only reproduce sexually we must reproduce and bring forth children in every way that is possible. We must create a legacy beyond our children. We must bring forth of our kind in others.

Who will you take with you? Who will you help to grow? Not the person who has already grown but the person who needs to grow.

Sometimes people boast about how they have helped someone who is already at the top. The person is already at the top. It costs you nothing to do something for them. Look lower down and let your gesture of goodwill cost you something.

Help someone with no access, no prestige, no way of paying you back except with a 'Thank You'. That is when you have made a difference. That is when you have multiplied yourself. That is when you are a faithful custodian of your gifts.

#talent

#mentor #reproduce

#legacy

#beyondmoney

#growpeople

#goodcustodian

10

SETTLE IN FOR A MARATHON

Men usually do this more times than women do: They see me running and then they start running-and they run very fast. They take off at top speed.

I notice, however, that even before they get halfway round the circuit they have tired out and start walking. Meanwhile I am running at a steady pace which I can handle, and I keep going for longer.

This is because first, they have not built up a habit of running. This is an occasional occurrence or just a happening at that moment.

Occasional happenings are just that: Like someone with an idea which they start and drop off quickly. They do not last. There is no stamina for the long run, no resilience to keep going when the going gets tough.

Secondly, they are doing it to show off. It never pays because the focus has come off yourself, what you need to do and why you are out running in the first place.

Since the motivation is wrong it is usually not a surprise when they cannot keep going. There is no truth in the action they have undertaken.

Finally, they stop because they have chosen to run at a pace which is unsustainable for them. The race is a marathon. It is not a sprint.

Choose a pace that suits you and settle in for a marathon.

#paceyourself

#gofurther

#itsamarathon

#focusonyourrun

11

FIND TIME FOR SOLITUDE

I tend to run alone. I know there are running clubs, but I have never tried to join any. I am not denying the possibility of joining one at some point. I have only ever run a marathon once. I find no need to do any social running but that does not mean I will not do it in the future.

When I run, I enjoy the solitude. I enjoy the opportunity of being by myself with just my thoughts. I do not have to speak with anyone else. It's me and the trees and the wind and the occasional dog walker.

That is fine by me.

I get an opportunity to reflect and find answers to situations which might be challenging at the moment. I come up with new ideas. My thoughts are developed and mulled over and given life. I am at peace with myself.

We are social beings. We need people around us but sometimes we must make the time and space to be by ourselves. Solitude is very important for thought, reflection and growth.

My 11-year-old daughter loves to be with people. She always wants to do things with someone. I tell her quite often; 'you need to enjoy your own company. You need to be able to spend time with yourself. You do not always have to have people around you'.

In life there are times when being able to enjoy your own company is very important. People walk away, and you look around when you need them the most but find yourself alone. Learn to use that time to reflect, to strengthen you, to be better, to grow.

Find time for solitude. Find space for thinking in whatever way you choose.

#solitude

#reflection

#growinthesilence

12

BECOMING YOU

I love to run. I run at least five times a week for about forty-five to fifty minutes. If I don't run, then it means I have an early start at work or slept late or didn't sleep well. There just has to be a good reason for me to wake up and not go for a run. My body and mind crave this early morning routine.

It was not always this way. When I started running, a 5 minute run felt like I would die. I persisted and got used to that so I increased it to 10 minutes. I almost died there too but I persisted and then went on to 15 minutes and so on and now I can run for an hour if I want to, every day and hardly break a sweat.

This has taught me a few things;

1. I had to develop the discipline to wake up every single morning and run.

2. I had to consistently run. It had to be a habit and not something I did sometimes when I felt like it.

3. By doing numbers one and two, I increased my capacity to run for longer periods of time

4. By doing all three, my confidence that I can run grew. No one can tell me I cannot run for fifteen minutes or fifty minutes.

And applying this lesson to life is easy:

Discipline and consistency in whatever you do will lead to increased capacity to do whatever you do.

This leads to a growth in confidence to do what you do.

This confidence does not come from anything external. It's a silent steadfast knowing, that's grown and developed over time.

It is irrelevant who does not compliment you, who does not give you a job you know you can do with your eyes closed or who acknowledges what you do. It's a knowing that cannot be taken away.

Now mind you a professional runner can come up to me and teach me to develop my posture or my breathing or help me to run further and longer.

In the same way in life, we never stop learning. It is important to be open to learning, to growing, to increasing capacity.

This openness to learning stems from a knowing how far you have come and what you can do. It stems from having the discipline to consistently follow your given path and having the confidence and courage to accept more and push further.

To growth, to becoming You.

#discipline
#consistency
#confidence
#learning
#growth

13

GRANDMA'S LESSON

Running provides me with lots of opportunity to think and reflect on the past and find answers for the present and dream of the future.

On one such day I was reflecting on my childhood:

I remember how as children we would go and spend time with our grandmothers for the day or the weekend.

The grandmas would always send me out to buy something or the other—either from the shop or from someone's home.

Lesson one: The grandmas knew exactly what they wanted you to get. They explained clearly to you what you were to purchase. Don't buy something else.

Lesson two: The grandmas were always clear about the destination. They knew what they wanted and where to get it. So, they would be specific in where they were sending you to. Don't go anywhere else.

Lesson three: The grandmas were very specific with their money. They knew exactly how much the item they wanted cost.

They would give you the exact money or if they gave you more, they knew how much change you had to bring back.

If you dared to drop a penny you had better be ready to bend down in the street and run your hands through the sand looking for that penny. Don't lose grandma's money.

Lesson four: the grandmas knew exactly how long it would take you to go and get what they wanted.

You were expected back within a specific time. You better not stop to talk to any friends on the way because they were waiting. Don't' dilly daly.

As I laughed at these memories, I realised how important they were to life.

Lesson one: God knows exactly why you are on this earth and what your mission is. God is specific about what you are supposed to do. Understand what it is that you are expected to do and go for it. Don't deviate from what is required of you.

Your mission has not been set by another human being.

Lesson two: God knows the way to get to where you need to go. Pay attention to spiritual directions and focus on the road you have been set on.

Another human has not set your destination they cannot tell you the way to get there. It does not mean you do not have mentors or learn from others who have succeeded in what you want to do.

Like Jim Rohn, says 'Listen to advise but make your own decisions. Take direction but not orders'.

Lesson Three; God knows what it will cost you to achieve your mission. The price you will have to pay is already determined, and you have been given exactly all that is required to acquire it. You are missing nothing. You have what it takes to fulfil your mission.

No human being put in you what is required because they did not send you out in the first place.

Lesson Four: God knows exactly how long you have to accomplish your mission. You are working at the pace required of you.

No man knows how long it will take you. No man sent you and so they cannot determine how long it will take.

Let each man go at the pace that has been set for them and accomplish their own mission.

#focusonthemission

#youhaveallittakes

#trustthevoiceinside

#besingleminded

#gogetit

14
RESULTS

When I weighed 85Kg and started running. I slowly started to lose the weight. It did not happen immediately. It took at least a year for me to start to see the weight go down in any significant way.

From there I knew that if I put on weight I did not want 10 days of running for an hour a day would get me back to my desired weight. Of course, eating right helps.

The issue here is that through running I can see the physical results on my body weight. I like these results, so I stay motivated to keep running.

The same goes for working. You will see the results. It might take a while for some. It might be quick for others. However much or less time it takes, there will be visible results you can see. As you see the right results start to happen, the more motivated you are to do more and your confidence grows and you are spurned on to do more.

#keeprunning
#results
#staymotivated

15

SET THE PACE

When I start to run, I decide on my pace. I do not want to run so fast that I burn out. I do not want to run so slow that I might as well be walking.

I need to run at a pace which allows me to have the exercise my body needs.

At the same time, I need to run at a pace which does not stop me from finishing my run because I am out of steam.

Thus, I must have a balanced pace.

It is irrelevant who is walking slower or running faster than me on the track. I have a focus; I know my capacity and so I pay attention to my pace to ensure I achieve my objective.

It's like driving in Milton Keynes where we have so many roundabouts.

A car can zoom past you and then you arrive at the roundabout and there they are, waiting. Their fast pace is irrelevant. You are both at the same destination.

Business and life are the same. You need to set a pace which works for you. Do not set a pace which is in comparison to others.

Decide what works for you; what will ensure that you can go on this journey for the long haul and not tire out or give up midway: What will ensure that you do not move too slow it's as though you are standing still.

Life is however, about learning and growing. Be open to changing the pace when you know better, when you get stronger, when you learn something new, when your capacity increases, you can increase your pace.

Be open to slowing your pace down when you need to; to protect your mental and physical wellbeing, to spending time with your family, to having fun, to learning new things.

#paceyourself

#knowyourpace

#learn #grow

#increaseyourcapacity

#focusonyourrace

16

WHO'S WATCHING

When I run, I am answerable only to myself. No one can see if I walked part of the way or all the way. I can say I run all the way and no one will know otherwise.

All that anyone has is my word that I just run for sixty minutes and didn't stop once.

It's the same with business. No one can see if I lied or cheated on a form. I am the only one who knows.

It is my job to hold myself accountable. To be a person of integrity.

Sometimes people say something or write it on social media, and I look at the way they behave or what they do and the two are in such opposite directions to each other.

I just wonder: is that the same person? Are they listening to themselves? Do they believe what they are saying or is it just the clichéd thing to say? Are they just playing the game to be popular with others? Are they just saying what others want to hear?

Then, I have to turn around and ask myself the same questions: Is what I am saying the same thing as what I do? Do I listen to myself? Am I true to myself?

Being who you say you are in private and public matters.

#Integrity
#truth
#beyourself
#betruetoyourself

17
THE PRICE

There is a price to pay for running. In the morning when sleep is at its sweetest and the bed is the warmest and cosiest place to be, I still have to get up and run.

I have to pay the price of foregoing my comfort for the cold and the inconvenience of getting up early.

I am willing to pay this price only because I know the reward is worth having at the end.

It is the same with business. There is a price to pay. I have to forego some things.

I have to wake up at 2am or 4am to work on a project. I have to stay at work longer than most.

I have to do more for the client. Offer more value than I am being paid for. My workload can be terribly heavy at times.

Yet I know I have to do them: I have to pay the price that is asked of me because I know the rewards will be worth it in the end.

#paytheprice

#keepgrinding

#itsworthit

#domore

18

CONFIDENCE BOOST

There is something empowering about getting up in the morning and going for a run.

I feel like I am capable of more. Most people are asleep but I am up early and running. Or it might be on a Sunday and most people are having a lie-in, but I am out running.

It boosts my confidence and sets me up for the day. I feel I can face anything. I am energised. Adrenaline is pumping.

I have not given way to comfort and ease. I have shown discipline.

I take this attitude into work with me. I feel I can do more. I am confident. I can offer more value to my client and associates. I am capable of doing the work and I am disciplined.

#discipline

#confidence

#domore

#pushyourself

19

THE NAYSAYERS

One interesting thing I have experienced from running is that some people who don't run do not want you to run either.

On one occasion a woman actually yelled at me 'you just need to eat right. You don't have to run'.

Beware of people who try to discourage you from the pursuit of your dream or vision. They are usually sitting down comfortable in whatever situation they are in, whether they are winning or losing, unable to see the point of your dreams.

It is so important to protect your vision from people who will seek to belittle it because they cannot imagine if for themselves.

Move to the other side of the track or turn your back and keep running.

#keeprunning

#walkawayfrom
naysayers

#hatecomfort

20
KICK THE CLICHÉS

I live on a council estate. It is one of the early estates built when Milton Keynes was first created as a city just over 50 years ago.

The houses here are over forty years old and look run down and neglected.

One thing I have noticed is that I never meet other people running.

I run five times a week so that is quite often and yet I will not meet one person on the run.

On the other hand, ten minutes in an affluent area and I will come across people running, morning, afternoon or night.

It just makes me wonder why: It costs nothing to walk or to run.

This I believe is a mindset.

It is so easy to give up on yourself when you have no money or society tells you that you are less than because of where you live.

Additionally, we do not see the right behaviours around us. People do not run around here.

What then happens is that we are not motivated to adopt

these good behaviours because we do not see others do it.

This is something to resist. Be more than what you have or where you are. The subject of my first book Professor Lynch said *'The place does not make the man. The man makes the place'.*

The same applies when it comes to education or work or being a high achiever. I am a high achiever, and I am a workaholic. It would be easier to settle and work in a warehouse for the rest of my days because that is what my environment dictates.

Not me: I have a Master's degree, I have sent in my proposal for my PhD research, I am running a successful business and this is my third book.

When no one around you is doing the right thing or the best thing or the high thing, where do you go for motivation?

We must go inside ourselves. We must create the ambition and the motivation and know for ourselves what is right and pursue that: For ourselves and for our children.

Kick the clichés in the teeth. Go run. Go be awesome.

#running

#feelbetter

#bebetter

#aimhigher

#changethenarrative

#changeyourmindset

#beamazing

21

YOUR BIGGEST CHEERLEADER

When I run, I do so on my own. There are no crowds to clap for me and cheer me on. There is no one on the sidelines telling me I am doing an amazing job: I have just one lap to go and should keep going. There is no one to hand me a bottle of water when I start to wane.

In life I am on this race on my own. It is irrelevant that others are running their own race, I am on my own.

I do not have to seek validation that I am doing well. I do not have to seek approval to keep running or moving or working.

I have to be self-motivated enough to run when no one cheers or says 'well done'.

It is always a nice thing to have people cheer you on but if you get addicted to people's approval you will be disappointed when it does not come.

So, learn to cheer yourself on.

Be your biggest Cheerleader.

#cheerleader
#selfmotivation
#keeprunning

THE BONUS TRACK
GROW IN THE PAIN

On several occasions I have seen people who stop running after going one lap or half a lap: It hurts or they are tired and so they stop running.

They do not realise that if they kept running, the pain would subside.

The parts of the body which hurt are proof that your body is stretching and working and changing to give you the results you want.

It's the same in life or business or any endeavours we undertake. We must never make this mistake and stop running.

It can hurt really bad: it can all look hopeless, but you have to stay in the race. There is no way of finishing or winning the race if you quit because it hurts now.

My 11-year-old daughter recently switched gymnastics clubs where she had to attend practice for sixteen hours instead of the six hours she was accustomed to.

She cried and complained that she no long wanted to go because her body was stretched and it hurt.

My advice was *'yes it hurts, do it anyway. Feel the pain and still push through'*.

Remember the growth is in the pain.

#keeprunning
#Dontstop
#thepainalways
passes

BONUS TRACK
DON'T STAY THE SAME

After running for a while it gets easier. Your body gets used to running and it hurts less. I am at a point now where running is enjoyable and not a thing I 'must do'.

This means I can run for longer and I can increase my pace. I am no longer in the same space I was when I first started running and five minutes felt like hell.

Life is the same, we grow and we change and we hopefully get better.

We must never stay the same. We must always strive to get better and do better.

When we have people in our lives with the complaint 'you've changed' or 'I want you to be the way you were', it's definitely time to move away from people like this who do not grow and don't want you to grow,

#growthmindset

#changeisgood

#notthesameperson

ABOUT THE AUTHOR

Nana Ofori-Atta Oguntola is a filmmaker and producer who loves to tell stories, especially stories of under-represented people and groups.

She holds a BA Hons degree in TV, Drama and Theatre studies from the University of Winchester and an Executive MBA in the Creative Industries from Ashridge Business School, HULT.

Her passion is telling stories which inspire other people to be and do better and above all to believe in their dreams.

She has produced a large catalogue of film and TV content and runs a training organisation in media and filmmaking. She provides consultancies in film and TV production and provides training for producers.

Printed in Poland
by Amazon Fulfillment
Poland Sp. z o.o., Wrocław

88155487R00045